LEADSPACE LEADERSHIP®

Your Energy in Motion to Lead with Clarity

DR. CAESAR KELLUM

Leadspace Leadership®: Your Energy in Motion to Lead with Clarity

First Edition – 2026

Published by:
Kinetic Leadership Consulting & Services, LLC
www.leadspaceleadership.com
info@kineticleadershipconsulting.com
ISBN: 979-8-9948603-2-8
Printed in the United States of America

What Leaders Are Saying About Leadspace Leadership

"An inspiring action plan for leaders at every level. Dr. Kellum gives you a practical system that's useful at all leadership levels."

Brigadier General Daniel J. Orcutt, USAF, Retired – Senior Air Force Leader and Operational Commander, Command Pilot (F-15E, KC-10, HH-60, T-38, T-37)

"Kellum's Leadspace Leadership is a toolbox. Like a mechanic's toolbox, Leadspace is full of frameworks you apply as-required, like a screwdriver or hammer, each for a different need. And Leadspace is not theoretical: each framework's chapter ends with an apply-it-right-now set of questions to help you solve your real-world challenges. "Bravo-Zulu!", Caesar! That's Navy-speak for "fantastic work"! Leadspace will help you manage complexity and create clarity as a leader."

Cory Bouck, former Naval Flight Officer/Mission Commander, author of *The Lens of Leadership: Being the Leader Others WANT to Follow*

"Leadspace Leadership is a transformative guide that equips leaders with the tools to navigate complexity, build trust, and lead with clarity and purpose. Combining decades of operational experience with scholarly research, Dr. Caesar Kellum creates a practical interdisciplinary framework that is both accessible and potentially impactful for developing leaders."

David V. Day, Professor of Psychological Science and Leadership, author of *Developing Leaders and Leadership: Principles, Practices, and Processes*

"This book felt like I was sitting across the table from a leader who's been there, learned through his real-life experiences and now wants to help you lead with the confidence, integrity, and success that he attained. Perhaps what was most striking to me is that in an era of digital everything, this book reminds us that the most effective leadership is still deeply human."

Scott Cawood, CEO, WorldatWork, Global Authority on Total Rewards, author of *The New Work Exchange: Embracing the Future by Putting Employees First*

"Leadspace Leadership captures what we've always hoped leadership development could be – disciplined thinking, deep reflection, and practitionership. He has refined what leadership development truly means. Leadspace Leadership doesn't just teach principles – it shows you how to discover your best self."

Dr. George E. Walker, Senior Research Analyst of The Formation of Scholars: Rethinking Doctoral Education for the Twenty-First Century, The Carnegie Foundation for the Advancement of Teaching

"Dr. Kellum's authenticity is apparent and genuine. It's the perfect how-to book that you can open to any page and immediately find help. 'From One Leader to Another' is the best part. I found myself rushing through the chapters just to get to this part."

Sergeant Major Joshua K. Miller, USMC,
Command Senior Enlisted Leader

"Dr. Kellum's Leadspace Leadership reinforces what modern leaders must develop to succeed in unpredictable environments—perspective, adaptability, and the ability to build dynamic capabilities within teams. This work provides a meaningful storyline for special operators to capture and communicate how we build leaders to perform, decide, and lead when it matters most."

Dr. Colby Cook, Executive Leadership Scholar-Practitioner
and Naval Special Warfare Leader

"Healthcare leaders today aren't struggling with knowledge — they're struggling with connection, clarity, and sustaining their people through constant pressure. Leadspace Leadership speaks directly to that need. Dr. Kellum reminds leaders how to slow down, see their teams, and lead in ways that restore purpose and trust when the profession needs it most."

Jeff Jurinak, Vice President,
Workforce Solutions – Health First

"Crisis, disaster response, and emergency management professionals at every level will find this work most valuable as they prepare for the moments when leadership really matters. Caesar provides practical tools to help leaders think clearly, communicate intent, and align teams operating in high-stress environments. It is a must have for leaders in this arena."

Major General John E. Barnette, USA (Ret.), Ed.D., Former West Virginia Army National Guard Commander, Task Force Commander, Hurricane Katrina and Rita Recovery Operations

"Dr. Kellum's Leadspace Leadership scholar-practitioner experiences in high-stakes environments can translate perfectly to functional, actionable, and uncomplicated methods for college & university students. His work makes complex leadership principles sound simple, clear and understandable that I know can aid students in becoming high performing leaders while pursuing their degree."

Dr. Irvin Clark, Associate Dean Student & Strategic Initiatives, Florida State University Panama City (FSU-PC)

Dedication

To our amazing daughter Alyssa and my beauTIFul wife Tiffiney – your love, patience, and support make this work possible. Thank you for walking this leadership journey with me. Words cannot bear the weight of my sincere gratitude for God's grace and glory – to be amongst angels.

How This Book Can Help You

Leaders don't struggle because they lack intelligence, experience, or drive. They're struggling because modern environments move fast, shift unpredictably, and flood them with more information than they can possibly process. When everything feels urgent and noisy, even seasoned leaders lose their ability to make sense of what matters most.

Leadspace Leadership solves that problem.

Leadspace Leadership is built on the idea that clarity is the leader's true advantage—not position, not authority, not charisma. In every environment, from the operations room to the boardroom, leaders face the same challenge—to make sense of complexity when the noise is loud and time is short.

This book offers a scholar-practitioner framework for developing that clarity.

Through story, reflection, and applied practice, Leadspace Leadership guides you through three enduring principles of effective leadership:

Awareness—seeing what others miss.

Consideration—orienting yourself to Leadspace Leadership components.

Engagement—putting your energy in motion to transform awareness into critical action.

Across ten chapters—that include the PICTURE, FIRESIDE, DEBRIEF, CONNECT, BUILD, and DRIVE frameworks—you'll discover how critical thinking, decision-making, and problem-solving converge with relationships, responsibilities, and roles to form the foundation of effective leadership.

Through the lived journey of a young officer who grows into a mentor, this book invites you to discover your Leadspace Leadership—the mental and relational space from which you lead with purpose. It challenges you to pause, observe, and move with deliberate energy, creating clarity where others see only fog.

Because leadership is not found in the absence of chaos—it's discovered within it.

TABLE OF CONTENTS

FOREWORD BY

BRIG. GEN. DANIEL J. ORCUTT, USAF (RET.)

We've all had days that were extremely busy, but nothing was actually accomplished—endless meetings talking in circles, a crisis where information was unreliable and time was short. On the drive home, maybe you wondered, *did I make a difference today...or did I just survive the day?*

Leadspace Leadership: Your Energy in Motion to Lead with Clarity is a book that will help you answer those questions. This isn't about what leadership looks like to someone else. This book takes you on a personal journey of leadership inquiry—ask yourself:

> **How do I know if I'm being the most effective leader I can be?**

Caesar provides answers by offering a scholar-practitioner framework rooted in executive leadership research and forged by real environments—operations rooms under pressure, disaster-response efforts, executive leadership experience, and the everyday complexity where leaders work to make sense of the noise.

Through storytelling, this book demonstrates how you can lead by using frameworks to achieve clarity while understanding the reality of where leaders operate—where problems are ambiguous, timing is unforgiving, and people bring both strength and stress to the table.

A Word Before You Begin

There is a quiet honesty running through this book.

It never pretends that leaders are simply born or made.

It never suggests that courage means certainty or success in the field.

It never confuses charisma with credibility.

Instead, it asks you to do something more difficult and far more important: to see through the fog, acknowledge your leadership potential, and say,

"I can make sense of this. I can focus my energy—and the energy of those around me—toward developing clarity with the Leadspace Leadership perspective."

If you are willing to be mindful in these moments, **Leadspace Leadership** gives you the tools, the language, and the framework to make it real.

My encouragement to you is simple:

- Don't rush these pages
- Reflect on the questions
- Use the frameworks with your team
- Revisit what you learned when experiencing stormy nights and quiet mornings

When you complete this book, you will have more than ideas about leadership.

You'll have a deep desire to be the most effective leader you can possibly be by discovering your compass of Leadspace Leadership and putting your energy in motion to lead with clarity.

PROLOGUE

THE MOMENT BEFORE THE STORM

The hum of the operations room filled the air, steady but uneasy—the sound of machines working harder than they should. Rows of monitors flickered with maps and chat windows that meant everything and nothing at once. A storm was coming, though the real storm wasn't outside—it was within the room.

A young officer stood at the center, surrounded by the glow of the video-teleconference screen and the quiet press of expectation. His team waited. The data didn't line up. The information wasn't complete. The mission clock kept ticking.

He could feel the pressure—not from the task itself, but from the unspoken question behind every pair of eyes watching him: What now?

He stared at the map. Lines crossed like veins, flashing in and out as updates fed in. No clear path. No easy call. Only ambiguity—the very terrain of leadership.

He inhaled slowly. "Alright," he said, his voice low but clear. "Let's stop for a second."

Movement froze. The chatter quieted. Even the hum of the machines seemed to fade for a moment.

He stepped closer to the display, tracing the contours of uncertainty. "Here's what we know," he began, his tone measured. "Here's what we don't. And here's what we are doing about finding out."

It wasn't poetry. It wasn't brilliance. But in that moment, it was leadership—calm, deliberate, human.

The storm outside rumbled, echoing through the walls. But something in the room shifted. The air lightened, tension replaced by focus. The team leaned forward again, not because the problem was solved, but because their leader had found clarity—and shared it.

Hours later, when the operation had stabilized and the adrenaline had drained, the officer sat alone under the fluorescent glow of the corridor. The quiet was heavier now—but it wasn't emptiness. It was reflection.

He opened his notebook and wrote:

*"**How do I know** if **I am** a good leader, no really – how do I know…*

*Am I being **the most effective leader I could possibly be**…*

How can I be the best leader ever—right now?"

Not the most powerful. Not the most decorated. Just the best I can be—the most effective, the most aware, the most trusted when the fog thickens and others freeze.

He didn't know it then, but that question would define his life.

"How do I know if I am being the most effective leader I can possibly be….

How do I know?"

Over time, it would evolve into a new perspective, a way of seeing, a discipline that captures, communicates, and credentials one's leadership with clarity, confidence, and credibility.

It would become the Leadspace Leadership perspective, a scholar-practitioner framework towards putting one's energy in motion to lead with clarity.

CHAPTER 1

THE PICTURE CALL: THE ART OF CRITICAL THINKING

How leaders learn to see through the fog

The morning light spilled across the flight line, but inside the operations center, the air was still heavy with fatigue. Monitors flickered, the aftertaste of adrenaline lingered along with the faint smell of burnt coffee from the break room.

The storm from the night before had passed—but its weight still hung in the air.

The young officer sat at his console, shoulders square but mind restless. The decisions from last night played in his head like echoes—second guessing, replaying, dissecting. Every choice had made sense at the moment, but clarity, he now realized, was a fragile thing in chaos.

That's when his mentor walked in—calm, unhurried, and somehow untouched by the storm. The older man had the look of someone who'd seen enough chaos to recognize the pattern beneath it.

He put his coffee down.

"You're still fighting yesterday, aren't you?"

The young officer didn't answer right away.

"I keep thinking about each call I made," he said finally. "If I'd seen the full picture sooner."

The mentor smiled faintly.

"Ah. The picture. Let's talk about that."

The Lesson of the PICTURE Framework

The mentor walked toward the whiteboard on the wall—the same one that had been a wall of confusion just last night. He wiped the board's chaos of dry-erase markings with his sleeve and then said:

"Most leaders think clarity comes from getting more information," he began. "But that's only half the truth. You can drown in data and still not see. Clarity comes from *perspective—knowing where to stand to see the whole picture.*"

He turned and handed the officer a marker.

"Draw it."

The officer hesitated, then began sketching data points, lines, arrows—all the pieces he remembered.

"Now," the mentor said, "tell me what this means."

The officer froze.

"It's … everything we saw last night."

"No," the mentor said gently. "It's everything you remember. Which means it's filtered—by your stress, your fatigue, your fear of being wrong. Leaders must learn to see beyond that."

He erased half the lines and wrote the word *PICTURE* down the side of the board. Just like a weapons controller makes a "Picture" call.

"Each letter stands for a deliberate step in disciplined thinking," he said.

P – Purpose: Why does this moment matter? What outcome truly counts?

I – Issue: What's the core question or problem we're really trying to solve?

C – Concepts: What key ideas, standards, or principles are shaping how we think?

T – Time: What's urgent, what's important, how much thinking time do we actually have?

U – Underlying Assumptions: What are we taking for granted or believing without testing?

R – References: What sources, experiences, or people are guiding our interpretation?

E – Evaluation: How will we judge success, risk, and learning once this is over?

He capped the marker. "Critical thinking isn't about knowing more," he continued. "It's about walking yourself through 'a PICTURE' call before you move. That's how you slow the mind down when the mission speeds up."

The young officer nodded slowly while staring at the whiteboard, letting the words sink in.

A Memory from Training

That lesson reminded him of a field exercise years earlier—a time when everything went wrong because he couldn't slow down.

He'd been a lieutenant then, wired for action. The exercise simulated a lost-communication scenario with aircraft in contested airspace. He had less than a minute to make a call, vector them left or right. He chose left—confidently, instinctively, quickly.

But the problem wasn't speed. It was an assumption.

The "lost" aircraft wasn't lost at all. It was following a contingency route he hadn't checked because he thought he already knew the answer. His team reacted to his direction, and for five simulated minutes, the entire exercise dissolved into confusion.

Afterward, his instructor pulled him aside.

"You made the decision fast," he said. "But you didn't *think*. You reacted."

"I followed the data," the lieutenant protested.

"No," the instructor said. "You followed your bias. You saw what you wanted to see. That's not leadership, that's reflex."

Then, his instructor gave him a single piece of advice:

"Leaders don't just act. They learn to develop their PICTURE quickly in chaotic situations, they share their thinking quickly, with themselves and others."

Seeing Through the Noise

Even that memory had been less about being a great controller and more about leadership itself. The same dynamic plays out everywhere—in strategy sessions, crisis calls, even family conversations.

People rush to fill silence with certainty. But certainty isn't leadership—awareness is.

He'd seen executives make the same mistake, mistaking motion for progress. In one boardroom session, a group of leaders argued over numbers on a slide, debating forecasts that hadn't even been verified. Voices rose, frustration flared, and decisions were made in heat, not in clarity.

He watched silently until the debate burned itself out. Then he asked a single question:

"Are we solving the problem that exists—or the one we're afraid of?"

The room went quiet.

At that moment the pause was felt, it was leadership. It wasn't command. It was a question of clarity.

The PICTURE in Practice

Back in the operations center, he began teaching his team to think in PICTURE steps.

He started each briefing with one challenge:

"What are we seeing?"

Not *what do we think*, not *what should we do.* Just *what do we see?*

At first, the younger officers resisted. They wanted certainty—fast, clean, decisive. But he insisted:

"If we can't define the problem clearly, every solution will be noise."

Slowly, they adapted. They started pausing before reacting, testing assumptions, questioning patterns. The room began to sound different—less chaotic, more deliberate.

And when the next storm came—and it did—they were ready. Not because they had more data, but because they had discipline of thought.

The Mentor's Return

Months later, the mentor returned to visit the team. He watched quietly from the back as the officer—now more confident, more grounded—guided his people through a complex scenario.

Afterward, he smiled.

"You've learned to see through all of this," he said in a bewildered, sarcastic way.

The officer nodded.

"I learned to make a PICTURE call."

REVIEW & REFLECTION

Review: PICTURE Framework—The Art of Critical Thinking

Leadership begins with awareness—but awareness without structure fades. Using the PICTURE call framework gives leaders a way to turn ambiguity into disciplined sensemaking:

- **P**urpose: Is this our problem? Do we all know why we're here?
- **I**ssue: Is this for information or is there a decision to be made?
- **C**oncepts: Are we in rescue mode or recovery?
- **T**ime: Is this Now, or the Next 24 hours? Who's got the clock?
- **U**se of Assumptions: What are the assumptions and facts?
- **R**eferences: Have we referenced those who may disagree?
- **E**valuation: How do we select a course of action for what's next?

Critical thinking isn't about looking smart. It's about being ready—ready to see the whole PICTURE when others see fragments.

This is the first component of discovering your Leadspace Leadership.

Reflection Questions: PICTURE in Motion

These questions are designed to help you move through *Awareness → Consideration → Engagement* as a leader.

Awareness: What Are You Actually Seeing?

Think about a recent situation where things felt unclear, rushed, or misaligned.

What part of the situation felt most obvious to you—what may have been explored about the larger picture?

____

____

____

Awareness thrives when leaders distinguish between what is visible and what is truly understood.

Consideration: How Are You Shaping the Picture?

Now reflect on your role in that same situation.

How did your mindset, authority, or emotional state shape the way the situation was framed—for you and for others?

____

____

____

Consideration requires leaders to recognize that they are part of the picture, not outside it.

Engagement: How Will You Create Clarity in Critical Thinking?

Revisit the situation using the PICTURE framework intentionally.

What would you pause, test, or reframe before acting if your goal was clarity rather than speed?

____

____

____

Engagement turns insight into action by choosing to create clarity before momentum takes over.

From One Leader to Another—What I Want You to Remember

I have been in rooms where the screens were full, the voices were loud, and the pressure was real—and yet clarity was completely absent. I've watched highly capable people talk past one another, not because they lacked intelligence or commitment, but because no one slowed the moment long enough to truly see what was happening—seemingly meaning the louder voice won that day.

In those moments, leadership is not about having the right answer. It's about having the discipline to pause, to orient, and to say, *"Let's make sense of this before we move."* That pause in time—uncomfortable as it may feel—is often the most decisive act a leader can take.

The PICTURE framework comes from those moments. It was forged in environments where time was short, information was incomplete, and people were waiting for directions. I learned that when leaders rush to action without clarity, they don't just risk poor decisions—they shape confusion, create tension, and misalignment that others must carry forward.

What I want you to remember is this: Clarity is not something you wait for—it is something you create. You are never separate from the situation you are trying to understand. Your presence, your energy, and your assumptions are always part of the picture. When you slow yourself down enough to see that clearly, others begin to see more clearly as well.

Critical thinking is not an academic exercise. It is a compass of leadership responsibility. And once clarity is navigated with critical thinking, leaders must decide how to act within it—because seeing clearly is only the beginning of leading effectively.

CHAPTER 2

THE FIRESIDE CHAT: DECISION MAKING UNDER PRESSURE

Sitting beside the heat of a decision without burning up

The operations room was darker this time. Only the back-lit glow of digital maps broke through as light. A storm front rolled across the radar and mission planning revealed one constant theme: uncertainty.

Every decision tonight would ripple outward. Each call made would shape the next six hours, maybe six months. The young officer—no longer brand new but not yet seasoned—stood with his team, eyes fixed on a radar picture no one had ever seen. He could feel the thrum of adrenaline beneath the surface, that dangerous edge where alertness meets hyper vigilance.

That's when his mentor appeared beside him.

"Breathe," he said quietly. "You're not fighting the storm or the mission—you're fighting yourself."

The officer didn't answer. He was already replaying possible outcomes in his head: *What if I wait too long? What if I commit too soon?*

The mentor pointed to the display.

"Leadership decisions are never made in perfect clarity," he said. "They're made in what I call the fireside—where heat, tension, and purpose meet."

He motioned for them to step into the briefing room, picked up a marker and wrote one word across the board: FIRESIDE.

The Lesson of the FIRESIDE Framework

"Every leader," the mentor said, "faces their own fire—pressure, emotion, uncertainty. But great leaders don't fear the fire. They learn to sit with it."

He began to explain, one step at a time:

F – Find & Frame the Context

Define what kind of problem you're in: simple, complicated, complex, or chaotic. Frame the real situation before reacting.

I – Identify Your Individual Role

Clarify your decision authority and personal bias. Who are *you* in this moment, and what's expected of you?

R – Resources & Relationships

Gather insight, not just information. Who has experience or data that can sharpen your decision? Build quick trust loops.

E – Environment & Enterprise

Sense the operating climate—culture, politics, timing. Every environment bends decision logic, leaders must adapt, not ignore it.

S – Seek Perspectives

Bring in voices that see from different vantage points. Dissent isn't disruption—it's depth.

I – Include & Integrate

Weigh emotion and logic together. Feelings reveal buy-in, facts reveal structure. Balance both.

D – Decide & Do

Choose. Commit. Communicate clearly. Ambiguity at the top becomes confusion below.

E – Examine Effects

Once the decision is in motion, observe impact and feedback. Debrief, document, and adjust.

The mentor capped the pen and turned to the officer.

"That's the FIRESIDE. Eight deliberate actions, one purpose—to make sense of pressure without letting pressure make sense of you."

The Fire Within

Hours later, decision time came—a crucial choice about repositioning critical assets. Data was split, timing impossible, risk unavoidable. The officer stood still, heart pounding.

He heard his mentor's voice echo in his head: Find & Frame the context. Identify your role.

He grabbed his notebook.

"Alright," he said to his team, voice calm but firm. "Our intent is preservation—mission and lives. Risk: delay equals vulnerability. Input: two viable positions."

He looked around. "Options—simplified. One path defends resources. The other protects people. Which aligns with our intent?"

Someone spoke up. "Protecting the team sustains the mission long-term."

He nodded. "Then that's our decision, danger is too close, safety first."

He spoke it clearly, without hesitation: "Move limited resources to Alpha Grid, everyone else should remain in place and hunker down. Now."

No second-guessing. No over-explaining. Just clarity in motion.

Within minutes, tension transformed into coordinated movement. Orders executed. Channels synced. The team acted—not because they were commanded, but because they believed the decision was sound.

The Fireside Moment

When it was over, the mentor found him outside by the smoke pit fire, leaning against the rail, staring into the night.

"You made the call," the mentor said.

The officer nodded. "I didn't know if it was right."

"None of us ever do," the mentor replied. "But you knew it was aligned. That's leadership."

He tossed a small stick into the burn barrel, flames rising softly.

"This," he said, pointing to the fire, "is what decision-making feels like. Heat. Doubt. Illumination. Sit with it long enough, and it teaches you to decide with discipline, not impulse."

The officer smiled faintly. "Like a fireside chat."

The mentor nodded. "Exactly."

When the Fire Turns Inward

Years later, the officer found himself at a conference table, no longer in uniform but in a suit. The stakes were different—financial, organizational, reputational—yet the pressure felt the same.

Around him, executives argued over a failed marketing approach, millions at risk, morale fading. Voices clashed, logic battled ego.

He didn't argue. He waited until the fire burned long enough to reveal the truth. Then, calmly, he said, "We're making this decision from fear, not from intent."

The entire room stopped in a moment—all eyes were on him.

He walked to the whiteboard and wrote a single word: FIRESIDE.

He broke it down just as his mentor once had—framing, identifying, engaging, deciding. But his tone now carried experience.

"Pressure doesn't mean panic," he said. "It means purpose. The fire isn't here to consume you—it's here to clarify what matters most."

And in that moment, a boardroom became a fireside chat—the kind where real leadership is forged.

Review & Reflection

Review: FIRESIDE Framework—Decision-Making Under Pressure

Leadership under pressure isn't about suppressing emotion—it's about integrating it with reason. Using the FIRESIDE framework helps leaders transform tension into clarity through deliberate reflection and structured dialogue.

When the fire rises, stand by its side:

- **F**ind & Frame: What's the topic? Facilitate a group discussion and find common references of frameworks (i.e. PICTURE Call for Critical Thinking)
- **I**dentify the different domains at play and isolate items of interest for consideration
- **R**ely on rehearsal of concepts to reference current procedures
- **E**xamine the environment to explore with subject matter experts
- **S**eek diverse perspectives to summarize the big picture
- **I**nclusive ideas from all players
- **D**ecide how to develop social contracts to communicate concerns
- **E**xamine the outcomes and learn to move forward with awareness to adjust

Because true decision-making isn't about avoiding the heat.

It's about learning to breathe as a leader despite how hot it gets.

Reflection Questions: FIRESIDE in Motion

These questions are designed to help you move through *Awareness → Consideration → Engagement* as a leader.

Awareness: What Is Driving the Tension?

Think about a recent decision where emotions were present, stakes felt high, or time was compressed.

What was creating the heat in this decision—and what signals did that tension reveal?

____

____

____

Awareness begins when leaders recognize tension as information, not as an obstacle to overcome.

Consideration: How Are You Influencing the Conversation?

Now reflect on *how you showed up* in that moment.

How did your presence, authority, or urgency shape the conversation before the decision was made?

____

____

____

Consideration requires leaders to recognize that they are stewarding the conversation, not merely participating in it.

Engagement: How Will You Create Shared Clarity Before Deciding?

Revisit that situation using the FIRESIDE framework intentionally.

What would you surface, slow down, or invite into the dialogue to build shared clarity before deciding?

____

____

____

Engagement turns decision-making into a shared act of clarity, not a unilateral moment of authority.

From One Leader to Another—What I Want You to Remember

I have watched high-stakes decisions unravel not because they were wrong, but because the conversations that shaped them were incomplete. The tension was there. The signals were present. But no one paused long enough to bring clarity into the room before moving forward.

In moments like those, leaders often feel pressure to decide quickly—to resolve discomfort, to demonstrate confidence, or to keep things moving. But decisive leadership does not mean decisive silence. It means having the courage to engage in the conversation that others may be avoiding.

The FIRESIDE framework comes from situations where dialogue mattered as much as the decision itself. I learned that when leaders bypass conversation under tension, they may gain speed, but they lose understanding. And when understanding is lost, decisions rarely hold.

What I want you to remember is this: Decisions do not create clarity—conversations do. The quality of your decisions will always reflect the quality of the dialogue that shaped them. How you listen, who you invite into the conversation, and what you are willing to allow to surface will be the determining factor whether people leave aligned or merely compliant.

Decision making is not a test of authority. It is a measure of leadership presence. And once clarity is built through meaningful dialogue, leaders must turn their attention to solving the problems that remain—because clarity without action only delays progress.

CHAPTER 3

THE DEBRIEF MOMENT: SOLVING PROBLEMS THAT MATTER

Why reflection is not optional—debriefs save lives

The morning after the operation was always the hardest. The adrenaline was gone, but the consequences remained—like smoke that lingered long after the fire had burned out.

The young officer sat at the same table that had felt alive the night before. Now it was still. Coffee cups half full, notebooks scattered, silence thick. The mission had been a success—technically. The objective was met. But the cost had been higher than expected. Miscommunication. Missed timing. Fatigue.

And for the first time, he wasn't sure if "success" was the right word.

His mentor entered the room quietly and pulled up a chair. No clipboard. No reprimand. Just presence.

"Rough night?" he asked.

The officer exhaled. "We completed the mission, but it didn't feel right. We lost tempo halfway through."

The mentor nodded. "Then the mission isn't over."

The officer frowned. "No, we finished an hour ago, it's complete."

The mentor shook his head. "A mission ends when you learn from it—not when you finish it."

He slid a small notepad across the table. Written across the top in thick, deliberate ink were seven letters: DEBRIEF.

The Lesson of the DEBRIEF Framework

"Most people," the mentor began, "think problem-solving is about fixing. It's not. It's about understanding. You can't fix what you don't understand—and you can't understand without reflection."

He flipped the page and began explaining each step:

D – Discuss the Event

Open the conversation. Name what happened in plain language. Authentic dialogue begins where defensiveness ends.

E – Establish the Facts

Strip away emotion and assumption. What *actually* occurred—actions, timing, sequence, outcome?

B – Bridge Perspectives

Every team member experienced a different version of the same moment. The truth lives in the overlap.

R – Reflect on Impact

Who or what was affected? What changed—energy, trust, tempo, performance?

I – Identify Lessons

What do we now know that we didn't before? What patterns keep showing up?

E – Empower Action

A lesson not applied is just a memory. Turn insight into next steps.

F – Follow Through

Reflection without accountability fades. Reinforce lessons until they become a habit.

He closed the notebook.

"This," he said, tapping the page, "is how leaders solve problems that matter—not with speed, but with sense."

The Cost of Unsolved Problems

This lesson was soon tested. A routine operation went sideways. Communication delay. Misdirection. No injuries—but the near-miss left everyone rattled.

That night, the officer gathered the team for a debrief. At first, no one spoke. The air was weird with quiet defensiveness—that complex blend of pride and guilt.

He began calmly. "We're not here to blame. We're here to understand."

He wrote DEBRIEF across the whiteboard.

"Let's start with the first D—Discuss the Event. What happened?"

Silence stretched until a sergeant finally spoke. "I assumed Alpha Team had already received the new corridor coordinates."

"They didn't," another added. "And I didn't confirm."

"Good," the officer said. "No judgment. Just the truth."

They worked through the rest of the framework—establishing facts, bridging perspectives, reflecting on the ripple effects.

By the end, the tension had lifted. Not because the mistake was erased, but because it had been understood.

From the back of the room, the mentor nodded. "You see?" he said later. "Reflection doesn't erase mistakes—it refines leaders."

The Power of Reflection Over Reaction

Later, the officer sat at a corporate conference table surrounded by project managers, analysts, and executives. The stakes were still high—only the uniforms had changed.

The discussion turned tense. A product launch had failed. Money was lost. Blame filled the air.

He waited until the noise peaked. Then, quietly, he said, "We're reacting. Let's reflect instead."

He stood and wrote DEBRIEF on the whiteboard.

A few eyebrows lifted—executives weren't used to simplicity. But he walked them through it anyway.

"Discuss what failed—not everything, just the core event."

They named three tangible contributing factors.

"Establish the facts—what really happened?"

Timelines replaced opinions. Facts replaced speculation.

"Bridge perspectives," he said. "Every department saw something different. Let's find the overlap."

Gradually, the tone shifted from accusation to curiosity.

By the time they reached Follow Through, they had a plan—rounded not in damage control, but in shared understanding of a debrief focal point.

When the meeting ended, one executive turned to him and said, "You just turned a crisis into a classroom."

He smiled. "That's the point."

When the Problem Is the Leader

This reminded him of facing a harder truth—something the team debrief couldn't solve. The problem wasn't the system, the mission, or the team communication. It was him.

He had been pushing his team too hard, expecting flawless execution without acknowledging fatigue. Productivity had become performance. Performance had become pressure. And under pressure, trust had begun to erode.

That night, he opened his notebook, he needed to debrief again—not the mission, but himself.

D – Discuss the Event: I've been leading with expectation, not empathy.

E – Establish the Facts: Missed cues. Short tempers. Low morale.

B – Bridge Perspectives: Team feedback—honest, raw, humbling.

R – Reflect on Impact: My leadership drove results—but at the cost of trust.

I – Identify Lessons: People don't follow pressure. They follow purpose.

E – Empower Action: Recommit to presence over performance.

F – Follow Through: Lead with rhythm, not rush.

The next day, he called his team together.

"I've been focused on performance," he said plainly, "but I lost sight of presence. That's on me."

There was no applause. Just quiet acknowledgment—and the start of something better.

REVIEW & REFLECTION

Review: DEBRIEF Framework—Solving Problems That Matter

Problem-solving isn't about intelligence—it's about humility.

The DEBRIEF framework turns every failure, frustration, or flaw into fuel for growth:

- **D**iscuss problems openly – no rank, no position, identify players with data
- **E**stablish what went well and what went wrong
- **B**ridge ideas about contributing factors that led to outcome
- **R**eflect on the opportunity to identify shortcomings and refine contracts
- **I**dentify key takeaways from data discovery and discussion
- **E**mpower one debrief focal point from all the factors – identify one thing
- **F**ollow up on action items and implementation of new innovations

The young officer learned that leadership maturity doesn't come from avoiding mistakes—it comes from processing them.

That's the essence of Leadspace Leadership: clarity born from reflection, motion guided by meaning.

He would carry that notebook for years—pages filled not with victories, but with lessons.

Because leaders aren't remembered for being perfect.

They're remembered for making the team better.

Reflection Questions: Debrief in Motion

These questions are designed to help you move through *Awareness → Consideration → Engagement* as a leader.

Awareness: What Problem Are You Actually Facing?

Think about a recent situation where a problem persisted, resurfaced, or grew more complex over time.

What caused the problem and where is your time and energy well spent to develop a focal point for a fix?

____

____

____

Awareness begins when leaders distinguish multiple contributing factors between what has happened and what's a debrief focal point for improvement.

Consideration: How Are You Framing the Problem for Others?

Now reflect on how *you* influenced the problem-solving effort.

How did your framing of the problem influence whether people reflected honestly or protected themselves?

____

____

____

Consideration requires leaders to recognize that the way a problem is framed often determines whether people are involved, for the problem to be solved.

Engagement: How Will You Learn to Debrief as a Fix?

Revisit the situation using the DEBRIEF framework intentionally.

What would you deliberately slow down, surface, or revisit to turn this problem into learning before fixing it?

____

____

____

Engagement turns problem solving into a learning discipline, not a reaction to pressure.

From One Leader to Another—What I Want You to Remember

I have seen organizations work tirelessly to solve problems—only to find themselves facing the same issues again, just under different names. The effort was real. The intentions were good. But learning never fully occurred.

In high-pressure environments, leaders are often rewarded for fixing problems quickly. Action feels productive. Reflection can feel like delay. But without learning, problem solving becomes a cycle of repeated lessons observed, not lessons learned.

The DEBRIEF framework comes from moments where leaders needed more than solutions—they needed understanding. I learned that when teams move forward without reflecting on what happened, why it happened, and what can be learned and improved—the problem is simply carried with them into the future.

What I want you to remember is this: Problems are not resolved by action alone—they are resolved through deliberate learning. Debriefing creates the space where insight replaces assumption and experience turns into wisdom. When leaders make learning visible, teams gain the confidence to adapt rather than repeat.

Problem solving is not about eliminating mistakes. It is about extracting meaning from those mistakes and calling it experience. And once leaders learn how to do that well, they are ready to take responsibility for connecting in relationships, building responsibilities, and driving their roles as a team.

CHAPTER 4

THE POWER TO CONNECT: BUILDING RELATIONSHIPS THAT ENDURE

Trust as infrastructure. Teams as energy systems, not org charts

The rain outside the command center came in thin sheets, streaking the glass walls and drumming lightly against the metal awning. Inside, the tension was heavier than the weather. Two departments, one mission—and nothing but friction.

The officer, now several years into his leadership journey, could feel it long before anyone spoke. The air itself carried it—clipped tones, half-finished sentences, eyes that didn't quite meet. The mission wasn't failing because of tactics or intelligence. It was failing because people had stopped trusting each other.

He leaned forward in his chair and looked around the table. Engineers sat across from logisticians. Analysts on one side, operators on the other. All brilliant. All tired.

"Before we talk operations," he said quietly, "let's talk connection."

Half the room looked puzzled, the other half skeptical.

He stood and wrote one word on the board in large, deliberate strokes:

CONNECT.

The Lesson of the CONNECT Framework

He turned back to the room. "If we can't connect, we can't coordinate. If we can't coordinate, we can't succeed. This isn't about orders—it's about trust."

He began writing down the letters:

C – Connecting

Seek common ground first. Find what unites before addressing what divides. Connection begins with presence, not persuasion. Connect with each other on some level.

O – Opening Dialogue

Create a safe space for authentic conversation. Ask instead of assume. Dialogue is the oxygen of trust.

N – Need for Relationships

Understand no complex problem can be solved without all of us contributing.

N – Navigating working together.

Turn "my plan" into "our process." Collaboration is co-creation, it turns resistance into momentum.

E – Empathic Consideration

Shift focus inward before pointing outward. Reflect on your tone, timing, and impact. Respect begins where ego ends.

C – Taking the Lead through Collaboration

Leadership is not control—it's communication of energy. Model the behavior you want multiplied.

T – Thrive Together

Celebrate collective progress. Shared success strengthens every bond that built it.

He set the marker down. "This isn't soft stuff," he said. "It's structural—the framework that carries the weight of everything else we do."

The Friction

Silence. Then someone from logistics finally said, "With respect, sir, we don't have time for this. We're behind schedule."

The officer smiled slightly. "That's exactly why we need this. The more pressure we face, the more connection we need."

He walked to a side table and picked up two identical cables. "These," he said, holding them up, "are both designed to transmit power. But this one—" he tapped it lightly "—is frayed. The power still moves through it, but it loses strength along the way. That's us right now."

He dropped the damaged cable. "Connection isn't just some cool buzz word—it's conductivity."

The room was just quiet enough to hear someone chuckle nervously, as some gasped aloud. Another nodded.

"We don't have a communication problem," he continued. "We have a connection problem. And the only way to fix it is to rebuild trust."

The Bridge Exercise

He paired members from different departments and gave them one rule: rebuild the mission plan using only questions—no directives, no corrections.

At first it was awkward. Engineers asked logisticians about timing, operators asked analysts about constraints. Voices softened. Curiosity replaced defensiveness.

And then, somewhere between the questions, they started listening to each other.

After thirty minutes, the room felt different. Energy was moving again. Ideas crossed the aisle. They weren't debating—they were designing.

The officer stood back, watching quietly. The frayed cable had begun to repair itself.

When they finished, he said simply, "That's the CONNECT framework in motion. You didn't fix the mission by working harder. You fixed it by getting closer, by connecting."

The Lesson Years Later

Years later, he sat in a corporate glass-walled boardroom high above the city. Different settings, same tension. Two senior vice presidents—finance and operations—arguing across the table, each certain they were right.

He didn't interrupt. He listened. He waited until it approached a point of no return, then said, "We're trying to manage numbers and emotions—what we really need to do is build trust."

The room went silent.

He stood and wrote the same word on the board: CONNECT.

"Let's run it," he said. "Just like we used to in the field." Nobody really knew how to react.

Yet, they walked through it together:

Co-production of ideas—none of us are as great as all of us

Opening dialogue without accusation

Need to explore each area of responsibility and role

Nurture relationships, because people matter

Examine any roadblocks or constraints

Consider only focusing on the positive

Take time needed to 'KNOW', not just say NO—bracket with [K]nowledge and [W]hy

When it ended, they didn't reach perfect agreement—they reached alignment through discussing a framework they could see.

"Connection," he said quietly, "isn't about everyone being the same. It's about everyone being seen and knowing we have something in common, we agree on more than you think."

The Story of Trust

A letter arrived from one of his old teammates:

Sir,

I didn't realize until years later that what you taught us wasn't strategy—it was humanity. You made us listen. You made us care again. And somehow, that made us better leaders in everything else.

He folded the letter and slipped it into the back of his notebook, right behind the first page that read, *What if I could be the best leader ever?*

That night, sitting by a campfire with his new team—no maps, no screens, just faces lit by flame—he said, "You can teach someone to follow procedures in a week. You can teach them to lead in a year. But to connect—that takes everyday heart."

He looked around the circle and smiled. "And that's why we're here. To lead—to connect."

Review & Reflection

Review: CONNECT Framework—Building Relationships that Endure

Using the CONNECT framework isn't theory, it's an infrastructure for trust. When relationships fail, missions fracture. When trust grows, energy flows.

To connect is to lead.

- **C**onnecting: Communicate commonalities, we have something in common
- **O**pening Dialogue: Observe relationships as interdependence
- **N**eed Exploration: Understand what empowers others to perform
- **N**avigating Co-Production: Collaborate toward shared outcomes
- **E**mpathic Consideration: Reflect inward to strengthen outward respect
- **C**ollaboratively Taking the Lead: Model trust in action
- **T**hrive Together: Because progress is never personal—it's collective

Leadership, he realized, wasn't about commanding people to move. It was about connecting them so they could move together.

The fire crackled softly in the night. And he remembered his mentor's words:

"You can't control the storm—but you can decide where you stand in it."
He looked around the circle and added quietly,
"And sometimes, the best way to stand—is together."

Reflection Questions: CONNECT in Motion

These questions are designed to help you move through

Awareness → Consideration → Engagement as a leader.

Awareness: How Are Relationships Showing Up Right Now?

Think about a recent situation where progress depended less on expertise and more on trust, influence, or collaboration with others.

Where is progress being limited by trust rather than capability?

____

____

____

Awareness begins when leaders recognize that relationships are always present—even when they are not being acknowledged. Think about where you can work on showing up more.

Consideration: How Are You Showing Up in Relationships?

Now reflect on *your role* within those relationships.

How do your actions and attention influence whether others feel seen, heard, or guarded?

____

____

____

Consideration requires leaders to recognize that trust is not assumed—it is built through behavior, not titles.

Engagement: How Will You Intentionally Build Connection?

Revisit the situation using the CONNECT framework intentionally.

What conversation or behavior would most strengthen connection and shared ownership right now?

____

____

____

Engagement turns relationships into a leadership capability, not a personality trait.

From One Leader to Another—What I Want You to Remember

I have worked with leaders who held impressive titles, deep expertise, and formal authority—yet struggled to move their teams forward. And I've worked alongside others who had little positional power, but whose presence, consistency, and trust allowed them to influence outcomes far beyond their role.

Leadership does not happen in isolation. It happens through people—through conversations, commitments, and the daily signals leaders send about what matters and who matters. When leaders rely solely on position, compliance may follow. But when leaders invest in connection, commitment emerges.

The CONNECT framework comes from moments where progress depended less on directives and more on relationships. I learned that when leaders overlook connection, they don't just weaken trust—they limit their ability to lead effectively through complexity, uncertainty, and change.

What I want you to remember is this: People do not commit to positions—they commit to relationships. Trust is built when leaders listen, follow through, and remain present when it would be easier to disengage. Connection is not soft leadership, it's durable leadership.

Relationships are not an accessory to leadership—they are the medium through which leadership works. And once leaders learn how to connect intentionally, they are ready to build shared responsibilities that move teams from alignment to execution.

CHAPTER 5

THE POWER TO BUILD: RESPONSIBILITIES THAT STRENGTHEN TEAMS

Ownership, purpose, and the shift from compliance to commitment

The hanger was thick with dust and diesel fumes that lingered in the air and filled the small, make-shift office set up to support operations. The mission had ended hours ago, but the work was far from over. Systems needed to be accounted for. Reports needed filing. A hundred small details that no one wanted to write into a situation report—but someone had to.

The officer stood near the open bay doors, watching his team move half-heartedly through breakdown. They weren't lazy. They were lost—unclear about who owned what, what came next, and why it mattered.

He could feel the drift. Responsibility had dissolved into routine.

His mentor's words echoed in his memory:

"Responsibility gives meaning and direction to energy.

He picked up a clipboard, looked at the task list, and knew what had to happen next. He called the team together.

They gathered reluctantly, standing in loose formation. Fatigue hung on every face.

He looked around, letting silence do the first bit of work.

"I know we're tired," he began. "But this isn't just about finishing tasks. This is about ownership."

He turned toward the whiteboard and wrote a single word across it in bold strokes:

BUILD.

The Lesson of the BUILD Framework

"Every leader builds teams," he said, "builds structure—not just buildings or weapons systems, but teams.

And the strength of a team isn't measured by how hard people work. It's measured by how clearly they know where they fit in the structure."

He wrote as he spoke, breaking down each letter:

B – Be Aware, Respectful, and Open

Awareness is the foundation of responsibility. You can't own what you don't see. Respect for others' work begins with understanding your own.

U – Utilize Abilities and Unite Strengths

Great teams don't hide talent in silos. They combine it. Recognize who can do what best—and trust them to do it.

I – Inspire Innovation

Responsibility isn't repetition of the same old way. It's evolution. Encourage people to adapt, to find better ways to serve the mission, not just repeat yesterday's success.

L – Learn Continuously

Every responsibility teaches something. If you're not learning, you're just laboring. Growth is the return on accountability.

D – Develop Collective Trust

Responsibility without trust is compliance. Responsibility with trust is commitment. Build agreements, not just assignments.

He capped the marker. "That's how you BUILD responsibility that strengthens teams," he said. "Not through control—but through clarity, connection, and commitment."

The Weight of Responsibility

A sergeant raised his hand. "Sir, with all due respect, we already have responsibilities and plenty of assignments."

The officer nodded. "You do. But what happens when the situation changes? When priorities shift?"

The sergeant hesitated.

"That's the problem," the officer said. "We confuse responsibility with routine. You can check a box without owning the outcome."

He pointed toward the equipment lined along the hangar wall. "Those systems don't get checked because it's policy. They get checked because lives depend on it. That's ownership."

The room fell silent—not from reprimand, but realization.

He handed out small cards with two questions printed on them:

1. What is my real role in the mission? (Ten words or less.)
2. Who depends on me doing it great? (Name two people.)

"Write your answers," he said. "Then we'll share."

The exercise was simple, but the effect was profound.

People began to articulate their purpose aloud:

The mechanic didn't just fix engines—he ensured mobility.

The analyst didn't just report data—she provided foresight.

The medic didn't just treat wounds—she protected readiness.

Purpose took shape through ownership.

The Rebuild

Later—after shift change, the officer and his mentor sat outside the hangar, the hum of generators fading into the quiet.

"You know," the mentor said, "leadership isn't about doing everything. It's about defining what must be done—and who will do it best."

The officer nodded. "I thought clarity came from structure. But it comes from trust."

"Exactly," the mentor said. "You don't build a team by giving tasks. You build it by gaining trust. Responsibility is how you teach people to lead themselves."

He paused, sipping his coffee.

"You're learning that accountability isn't control. It's a deeper connection."

The Corporate Parallel

The same lesson replayed—this time as a corporate board member.

The officer, now an executive, watched department heads circle around a problem no one wanted to claim. Budgets were late.

Deliverables were missing. Everyone was "waiting on someone else."

He stood and walked to the board.

"Let's make this simple," he said. "We have a BUILD problem."

He wrote it out just as before:

Be Aware. Utilize. Inspire. Learn. Develop.

"Let's start with the first one," he said. "Be aware—what's the real mission here?"

Someone murmured, "Deliver a better customer experience" and with more enthusiasm, added, "well above our competitors", she got louder, "we want to set the bar, to be the industry standard that everyone else is trying to catch up to."

"Good," he said. "We can use that. Now—who owns what?"

Silence. Then, one by one, people began to speak.

Responsibility mixed with enthusiasm started to surface.

By the end of the meeting, chaos had turned into coordination. Ownership had replaced friction.

As the room cleared, one senior manager stopped him.

"You didn't just assign accountability," she said. "You gave it meaning."

He smiled. "That's what using a BUILD framework does to leadership."

The Personal Reckoning

One evening, long after the office had emptied, he sat alone at his desk. The city lights shimmered below like stars that had traded sky for skyline.

He opened his notebook and wrote:

"Responsibility is how we show respect for trust."

"Ownership turns effort into excellence."

He thought of his team—then and now—and realized something deeper: Every strong mission, every culture, every relationship thrives on the same truth.

People don't want to be managed. They want to matter.

And when they understand how their responsibilities connect to the whole, they don't just perform—they lead.

Review & Reflection

Review: BUILD Framework—Responsibilities that Strengthen Teams

Using the BUILD framework transforms responsibility from obligation into empowerment:

- **B**e aware of individual abilities and respectful of their responsibilities
- **U**tilize the availability of other's abilities and knowledge
- **I**nspire innovative thinking and involve all players
- **L**earn to leverage the thinking of others through critical thinking practices
- **D**evelop social contracts to thrive and build trust

Leadership isn't about control. It's about clarity—clarity that builds confidence, competence, and community.

The officer had learned that every great team is *built*, not assigned. And the best leaders don't build followers.

They build more leaders.

He closed his notebook, stood, and looked out at the city once more. Tomorrow would bring another mission, another storm, another team depending on clarity.

But tonight, he smiled quietly, knowing that the structure he had spent years building wasn't made of steel or glass—it was made of trust.

Reflection Questions: BUILD in Motion

These questions are designed to help you move through *Awareness → Consideration → Engagement* as a leader.

Awareness: Where Does Responsibility Actually Live?

Think about a recent situation where expectations were unclear, accountability felt uneven, or work stalled despite good intentions.

Where did ownership feel strong, and where did it feel diluted or avoided?

____

____

____

Awareness begins when leaders recognize that confusion around responsibility often looks like a performance problem—but rarely is.

Consideration: How Are You Shaping Responsibility for Others?

Now reflect on *your role* in establishing responsibility.

How have your expectations, clarity, or tolerance for ambiguity impacted accountability across the team?

____

____

____

Consideration requires leaders to recognize that responsibility is not delegated once—it is shaped continuously.

Engagement: How Will You Build Shared Ownership?

Revisit the situation using the BUILD framework intentionally.

What responsibility needs to be clarified, aligned, or rebuilt to strengthen ownership and trust?

____

____

____

Engagement turns responsibility into a shared commitment, not a compliance mechanism.

From One Leader to Another—What I Want You to Remember

I have seen teams with talent, trust, and motivation still struggle—not because they lacked effort, but because responsibility was never fully built. Everyone was busy. Everyone was contributing. Yet ownership remained unclear, and progress slowed under the weight of ambiguity.

Leaders often assume responsibility will sort itself out once direction is given. But responsibility does not emerge from instruction alone. It develops when expectations are discussed, roles are understood, and teamwork is shaped through ongoing engagement.

The BUILD framework comes from moments where leaders needed more than alignment—they needed ownership. I learned that when responsibility is left vague, leaders end up carrying more than they should, while teams carry less than they are capable of.

What I want you to remember is this: Responsibility is not about assigning tasks—it is about building ownership. When leaders take the time to clarify expectations and align responsibility with trust, teams stop waiting for direction and start moving with purpose.

Responsibility is where connection becomes execution. And once leaders learn how to build it intentionally, they are ready to DRIVE in their roles.

CHAPTER 6

THE POWER TO DRIVE: ROLES THAT DEFINE MOTION

From planning to propulsion. How leaders create momentum on purpose

The dawn light crept over the flight line, stretching long shadows across the tarmac. The air was sharp, metallic, charged with potential—that tense stillness that exists right before executing a mission never tried before.

Inside the hangar, the officer walked the floor as his team prepared for a critical joint operation. Every checklist was complete, every unit accounted for. Yet he could feel it—that quiet hesitation that lives in the gap between ready and go.

He paused, watching a young technician fumble with a sensor calibration. It wasn't incompetence, it was again—uncertainty.

Leadership, he realized, didn't end when you gave direction.

It began when you created *drive.*

He motioned for the team to gather.

The Call to Drive

They circled around him, clipboards in hand, flight jackets half-zipped. He could sense their caution—the way people look when they know the plan but don't yet believe in it.

He smiled. "We've planned this mission down to every inch," he said. "But precision means nothing without energy to move. It's time to DRIVE our roles."

He turned to the whiteboard and drew five bold letters across the surface:

D – Develop Agreement

R – Represent Roles

I – Identify Dominant Discourse

V – Visualize Possibilities

E – Evaluate Effort

The Lesson of the DRIVE Framework

"Every mission," he began, "has two engines: clarity and momentum. Clarity keeps you aligned. Momentum keeps you alive. DRIVE keeps them both in sync."

He tapped the first letter.

D – Develop Agreement

Before you move, align on what "success" means. Agreement builds cohesion, and cohesion is what moves teams through uncertainty.

R – Represent Roles

Make sure every person knows what they stand for—and who they stand beside. When roles are understood, responsibility evolves into rhythm.

I – Identify Dominant Discourse

Every team runs on narrative. Listen to the story being told—is it possibility or pressure? Shift the story, and you shift the outcome.

V – Visualize Possibilities

Before you execute, see the paths ahead. Great leaders don't predict the future; they prepare the space where decisions can grow.

E – Evaluate Effort

Excellence isn't just achievement—it's awareness in motion. Measure progress by growth, not perfection.

He turned to face them.

"This is how we lead the mission instead of being led by it, DRIVE puts our mission in motion."

A Mission in Motion

The operation was launched that afternoon. What began as quiet hesitation turned into sharp focus. Radios clicked. Vehicles rolled. Aircraft lifted.

From the control tower, the officer watched the mission unfold like a living organism—coordinated, confident, moving with intent.

Then, halfway through, a package delay threatened to derail the timeline. The tension was instant.

"Stay on DRIVE," he said into the comms. "Develop agreement, re-align."

The operations lead responded immediately, grounding the team's DRIVE: "Our purpose remains—protect the route, preserve momentum."

The tone changed. The hesitation dissolved. They adjusted routes, redistributed loads, and kept moving.

The mission finished on time—not because every plan held, but because every person stayed *aligned* to drive.

Afterward, a young officer said, "Sir, you didn't tell us what to do when things changed—you showed us how to think when they did."

He smiled. "That's DRIVE. It's not direction—it's clarity and momentum."

The Corporate Translation

Years later, in a corporate setting, the same principle played out differently but felt the same.

The stakes were financial this time—a product rollout instead of a flight operation—but the symptoms were identical: competing priorities, communication gaps, and fatigue disguised as busyness.

The executive team sat around a polished table, staring at charts that told them nothing.

He stood and quietly wrote DRIVE on the whiteboard.

"Let's reset," he said. "Start with the D—Develop Agreement. What are we actually trying to achieve?"

Someone replied, "Launch our new platform by Q3."

He nodded. "That's a timeline. What's the mission?"

A pause. Then another voice said, "Empowering small businesses to grow."

He smiled. "That's it. Represent Roles—who owns what? Identify the narrative we're telling our people. Are we making them do the 'same ole' roles, is it burnout or do they believe in what we are doing?"

By the end of the session, the tension had transformed into alignment. People leaned forward. Ideas connected. The intent had regained motion.

When someone asked how he'd realigned them so quickly, he said,

"I didn't change the plan, I reconnected them to their role in motion to lead, with purpose."

The Mentor Returns

That night, long after the city lights flickered on, his phone rang.

The voice on the other end was familiar—steady, grounded.

"I heard about your company's turnaround," his mentor said. "Sounds like you've learned how to lead through alignment."

He chuckled. "You taught me that long ago—clarity and motion, awareness and energy."

The mentor paused. "And what keeps them connected?"

"Accountability," the officer answered instinctively.

"Not exactly," the mentor replied gently. "Alignment. Accountability is the measure—alignment is the motion."

He let the words settle.

"Just remember," the mentor added, "drive the mission, don't let the mission drive you."

Review & Reflection

Review: DRIVE Framework—Roles that Define Motion

Using the DRIVE framework transforms activity into alignment and effort into excellence. It turns execution from reaction into rhythm:

- **D**evelop a conversation about "what right looks like" to move forward
- **R**epresent and report your position on the subject
- **I**dentify the running story, making a shift may make a difference
- **V**isualize innovation and explore areas for expansion
- **E**valuate phases of approach for constant learning and evaluation

Leaders who DRIVE don't wait for the perfect plan; they create clarity in motion.

They don't command compliance—they cultivate conviction.

They don't chase outcomes—they align energy toward purpose.

That's the essence of Leadspace Leadership: energy, awareness, and alignment in motion.

Reflection Questions: BUILD in Motion

These questions are designed to help you move through *Awareness → Consideration → Engagement* as a leader.

Awareness: How Are Roles Actually Playing Out?

Think about a recent situation where work was moving, but coordination, ownership, or execution felt uneven.

Where is work moving well—but momentum slowing—because roles are unclear in practice?

____

____

____

Awareness begins when leaders recognize that unclear roles often show up as friction, delay, or duplicated effort.

Consideration: Are You Clarifying or Complicating Roles?

Now reflect on how *you* influence role clarity.

How does your direction, timing, or interventions shape how others understand and own their role?

____

____

____

Consideration requires leaders to recognize that roles are reinforced by behavior more than description.

Engagement: How Will You Drive Role Clarity in Action?

Revisit the situation using the DRIVE framework intentionally.

What clarity of roles may establish, reinforce, align and sustain momentum?

____

____

____

Engagement turns roles into a source of momentum, not confusion.

From One Leader to Another—What I Want You to Remember

I have seen capable teams stall not because they lacked talent or motivation, but because roles were unclear in the moments that mattered most. Everyone was doing *something*—yet no one was quite sure who owned what when decisions, timing, or follow-through were required.

Leaders often assume roles are obvious once responsibilities are assigned. But roles are not static descriptions — they are lived expectations that show up under pressure. When roles are unclear, leaders end up hovering and teams lose confidence in how to move without constant direction.

The DRIVE framework comes from moments when leaders needed coordination, not control. I learned that when roles are clear, teams move faster, communicate better, and trust one another's contributions. When roles are unclear, even the best intentions turn into hesitation or overlap.

What I want you to remember is this: Roles should not limit people—they should liberate them. Clear roles give individuals the confidence to act, decide, and contribute without waiting for permission. They turn their responsibility of role improvement into execution.

Roles are where responsibility becomes visible in action. And once leaders learn how to drive role clarity intentionally, they create teams that can sustain performance, adapt under pressure, and move forward together with purpose.

CHAPTER 7

ACT: AWARENESS IN ACTION

Awareness graduates into leadership

The drafting light spilled across the large mission planning cell briefing table, illuminating a map marked with arrows, grids, and circles of threats. The team sat ready—trained, aware, and aligned. But awareness alone had never changed the world.

The officer stood quietly, running a hand over the map's smooth surface. He had been here before—on the edge between knowing and doing. Between theory and action. Between what could be done and what must be done.

"Awareness is the spark," his mentor had once said, "but action is the flame."

He turned to his team. "We've studied the situation. We've analyzed every angle. But leadership doesn't happen on paper. It happens in motion."

He picked up a marker and wrote three bold letters on the board:

A – Analyze

C – Create

T – Test

"This," he said, "is how we begin turning awareness into impact."

The Lesson of the ACT Framework

Analyze.

"Look deeper than the obvious," he said. "Awareness without analysis is assumption. Every decision must be informed by what we know—not what we feel."

He pointed to a satellite image on the screen. "This is what's happening. But what's really happening beneath it? Where is the leverage point?"

They discussed, debated, and reframed. Awareness sharpened by shared analysis and understanding.

Create.

"Once you understand," he continued, "you must create. Leadership is not about reacting—it's about constructing clarity where none exists."

He assigned small teams to design quick solutions. They sketched, created, and built prototypes of ideas.

Test.

"Now," he said, "we add what we need more of and subtract what detracts from our energy and the mission. Because theory means nothing until it meets reality in practice."

They ran the options in simulation. Some worked. Some didn't.

No one got defensive. No one took it personally. This wasn't about who came up with the idea. It was about whether the idea would work under heat.

Within hours, their concept had transformed into an actionable plan. Not perfect—but progressing.

He didn't praise them for being right. He praised them for being *willing to move* but more importantly to act.

The Rhythm of Action

That night, after the mission succeeded, the officer sat in deep reflection. The distant flicker of stars were like waypoints—steady, patient.

He thought about how easy it is to stop at awareness—to talk, to analyze, to wait for perfect alignment. But perfect alignment is fantasy.

He wrote in his journal:

Awareness without action is observation. Awareness in action is leadership.

The ACT framework had given him a cadence:

1. Analyze what is.
2. Create what could be.
3. Test what works.

It was simple. It was repeatable. It built momentum. And momentum is what saves teams from paralysis.

Action, he realized, is not the enemy of thinking. It is how thinking becomes real.

When They Froze

Weeks later, his team hit a stall. Morale was low. Tempo was off. Initiative had quietly died.

Nobody said, "we're afraid." It showed up as something else: long pauses, late responses, doing what was asked and nothing more.

He called them together.

"We're going to run ACT right now," he said. "On us."

He drew three circles on the board.

ANALYZE — "What's actually happening with us right now?"

They answered. Honestly.

"We don't want to make the wrong move so we're not making any move."

CREATE — "What's a better way of working the next 48 hours?"

Ideas started surfacing. Smaller teams. Clearer drills. Less noise on comms. More face-to-face.

TEST — "Which one are we willing to try immediately?"

They circled one approach. They ran it for two days.

Performance came back online.

Not because pressure increased. Because clarity did.

He watched and thought, "This is it. This is what leadership is supposed to feel like. I'm not dragging them. I'm letting them move and act as leaders."

The Lesson He Didn't Expect

Later, one of his youngest Airmen caught him in the hall.

"Sir," she said, "thanks for letting us try something instead of telling us we were underperforming."

He paused.

"That's what you thought I was going to say?"

She nodded. "That's what most team leaders usually say."

He carried that with him for months.

Because in that moment, he understood that ACT isn't just a tool for mission design or a process. It's a way of honoring people's dynamic capabilities. It says, I trust you to grow and go with me.

That is the difference between directing and leading.

Reflection & Review: ACT—Awareness in Action

ACT is where awareness graduates into leadership.

Analyze—Name the reality without ego.

Create—Generate options without fear.

Test—Move in the real world without waiting for perfection.

Leaders who ACT don't hide in strategy ideas of visional success.

They step into time and space and move energy forward.

Because awareness with no motion is potential.

Awareness in motion is impact.

And that is the work of a leader.

CHAPTER 8

FACT: TURNING AWARENESS INTO CLARITY

Making the right decision in the middle of the storm

The tactical operations center was loud—too loud. Radios chattered. Fingers flew across keyboards. People spoke in fast, clipped phrases, some with two phones in different conversations. Everyone was working. No one was aligned.

The officer stood at the center of the frenzy, headset in one ear, his other hand braced on the edge of the table. Information was coming in from five directions, none of it made sense.

He could feel it in his lower back—the creeping locked up tension that comes not from danger, but from ambiguity.

That's when his mentor's voice from years ago echoed back:

"Awareness tells you what is happening. Clarity tells you why it matters."

He took a breath and stepped toward the whiteboard.

"Everyone stop," he said. "We're going to slow this down."

A few heads snapped toward him.

He uncapped a marker and wrote four letters in calm, steady strokes:

F – Frame the Decision

A – Assess the Environment

C – Choose and Communicate

T – Track and Transform

"This is FACT," he said. "We're using it now."

The Lesson of the FACT Framework

Frame the Decision.

"Before we can decide," he said, "we have to be clear on *what we're actually deciding.*"

He pointed to the map. "We're not deciding the whole mission. We're deciding where to move first support."

Heads nodded. He could see tension drop almost immediately.

He'd just done something subtle but enormous, he made the decision smaller.

Assess the Environment.

"What do we know for certain? What do we not know? What is changing?"

People began to report in a different way—less emotion, more precision. They stopped describing how they felt and started describing what was real.

Choose and Communicate.

He turned, voice calm. "Priority is sustaining the people who allow the mission to continue. Resupply Bravo. That's the call."

And here, he did the one thing too many leaders skip, he said it out loud, clearly and once.

Not, "I think maybe we should consider…"

But, "Here's the decision. Execute."

When leaders hesitate, teams fracture. When leaders declare, teams align.

Track and Transform.

"Now we monitor it," he said. "If the environment shifts in the next 30 minutes, we reassess and adapt."

Leadership was no longer a moment. It had become a loop.

The Storm Passed—the Lesson Stayed

After the tempo stabilized and the room settled back into an efficient hum, one of the techs approached him.

"Sir," she said, "that cut through the noise."

He nodded. "That's what FACT is for."

Later, alone, he wrote:

Clarity isn't found. Clarity is forged.

He realized something else that night, most teams don't struggle with talent. They struggle with alignment. And most leaders don't struggle with intelligence. They struggle with framing.

The difference between chaos and coordination is whether someone is willing to say:

"This is the decision we're actually making."

Boardroom Parallel

Years later, two VPs, one initiative, no agreement. Everyone in the room was talking, but nobody was leading.

He let it run for a few minutes and then, just like before, said, "Stop."

He walked to the wall and wrote:

F – Frame the Decision

A – Assess the Environment

C – Choose and Communicate

T – Track and Transform

"We're not deciding everything about next quarter," he said. "We're deciding this: Do we delay rollout by 30 days to protect trust, or do we stay on date and take the credibility hit?"

Silence.

That framing alone changed the entire tone of the room.

Because when there is no frame, people fight different problems and think they're disagreeing. Once you frame, they're finally in the same fight.

They assessed: What's factual? What's assumption? What's optics? What's truth? They chose: "We delay and over-communicate." They tracked: Daily credibility reports, not just numbers.

He didn't just "facilitate." He built clarity.

People later told him, "That was the first time this leadership team felt like a leadership team."

Reflection & Review: FACT—Turning Awareness into Clarity

FACT becomes the spine of decisive leadership.

- **F**rame the Decision—Define the real choice.
- **A**ssess the Environment—Gather what's true and what's shifting.
- **C**hoose and Communicate —Decide with conviction and share it clearly.
- **T**rack and Transform—Adapt based on outcomes, not ego.

Leaders who run FACT don't pretend to be certain.

They create certainty of direction.

That's what people actually need to follow.

Not perfection. Direction.

CHAPTER 9

IMPACT: REFLECTION AND LEGACY IN LEADERSHIP

Moving from "I led well today" to "I formed leaders who will outlast me."

The base had gone quiet.

The mission was over. The radios were silent. The night was still except for the slow, steady hum of the crickets in the distance.

The officer sat alone at a folding table with a stack of reports. Numbers, timelines, movements, outcomes. All the proof that the plan had worked.

But something in him resisted the word "success."

He pushed the stack aside and stared at his notebook.

"What was the impact?" he asked quietly.

Not: Did we hit the metric? Not: Did we check the box? But: What changed because we were here?

He wrote one word in block letters that took up half a page:

IMPACT.

Then he wrote down what would become his final leadership frame:

I – Identify the Intent

M – Measure the Movement

P – Pause for Perspective

A – Apply the Lesson

C – Communicate the Change

T – Transfer the Teaching

The Lesson of the IMPACT Framework

Identify the Intent.

"What were we actually trying to accomplish?" he wrote.

Not the task—the purpose.

Measure the Movement.

"What moved because of us?"

People, confidence, capability, readiness, trust—not just throughput and timing.

He realized something important: numbers matter, but effectiveness matters more.

Pause for Perspective.

He forced himself to sit in stillness. No rush to "what's next." Reflection is not wasting time. Reflection is where leadership cashes the dividends of experience.

In the silence, he noticed something he had missed in the moment: one of his younger Airmen had stepped up, taken initiative, and quietly stabilized a broken process without waiting for permission.

That mattered. That was scalable. That was leadership legacy in motion.

Apply the Lesson.

He wrote down three adjustments for the next cycle. Real changes. Not "we should," but "we will."

Communicate the Change.

The next morning, he gathered the team. He didn't just congratulate them. He told the truth. Here's what worked. Here's what we're changing. Here's why it matters.

People stood taller when they heard it. Not because it was praise. Because it was leadership.

Transfer the Teaching.

Finally, he pulled the young Airman aside. "You're going to teach this new process to the next rotation," he said.

She looked stunned. "Me?" "You," he said. "Because what you say has an impact!"

And that was the moment he understood.

Impact is not what *you* did. Impact is who can lead now, without needing you.

The Quiet Call

Years later, he would sit across from a young officer, as a senior mentor—the same way his mentor once sat across from him.

The much younger leader was shaken, exhausted, questioning himself in the after-action quiet.

And he would say, softly, "Do you know what you're missing?"

When the young officer didn't answer, he'd smile.

"Your Leadspace Leadership perspective."

In that instant, the circle closed.

He was the mentor now. He had become the steady voice in someone else's storm. And that, more than any metric, was his realization that he could now answer his life-long question about being an effective leader.

He hadn't just led missions. He had produced leaders capable of meeting the complexities of leadership.

Reflection & Review: IMPACT—Reflection and Legacy in Leadership

IMPACT is how you make sure your leadership outlives your presence.

- **I**dentify the Intent—Why did we act?
- **M**easure the Movement—What actually changed?
- **P**ause for Perspective—What did we miss in the rush?
- **A**pply the Lesson—What adjusts now?
- **C**ommunicate the Change—Who needs to hear it and why?
- **T**ransfer the Teaching—Who leads next?

This is the final realization of Leadspace Leadership:

You are no longer the center of control.

You are the source of courage.

And your test is simple:

If you walk away, does clarity stay, or does it walk with you?

If clarity stays, you're not just effective.

You're a leader.

CHAPTER 10

LEADSPACE LEADERSHIP: YOUR ENERGY IN MOTION

An Interdisciplinary Way of Seeing, Thinking, and Leading

The room was quiet, but alive. No radar screens. No generator hum. Just light spilling across whiteboards and notebooks, where leaders from every background leaned forward—a commander, a hospital administrator, a law partner, a nonprofit director, a student. Different missions. One shared question:

How do I lead clearly when everything feels complex?

At the front stood Dr. Caesar Kellum—a former enlisted weapons controller and intelligence weapons officer, now a scholar-practitioner of leadership. He smiled, picked up a marker, and wrote two words that defined his life's work:

Leadspace Leadership

"This isn't just another popular mechanics or gimmick of leadership improvement," he said. "It's an interdisciplinary way of seeing, thinking, and leading. It's how we make sense of complexity—and then move energy with purpose."

From Airspace to Battlespace to Leadspace Leadership

He drew three arcs on the board.

Airspace. Battlespace. Leadspace.

"When I was an aerospace control and warning operator in the United States Air Force," he began, we trained inside well-defined *airspace*—lateral, linear, and vertical boundaries of the National Airspace System. The missions were intense, the maneuvers complex, but the boundaries were known. Everyone shared the same picture."

He shaded the next arc.

"Later, as an intelligence weapons officer, my focus shifted to *battlespace*—the dynamic environment of threats, decisions, and human judgment.

It wasn't about coordinates anymore. It was about cognition. The battlespace demanded sensemaking—integrating information, applying tactics, understanding risk, and moving fast but wisely."

Finally, he circled the top arc.

"And then came *Leadspace* Leadership—the interdisciplinary theory of leadership development.

This is where you spend your energy to be the most effective leader you can possibly be—where clarity, consideration, and engagement converge."

He paused.

"In Airspace, you control precision.

In Battlespace, you coordinate complexity.

In Leadspace, you create clarity."

The group nodded. They could *feel* the transition—from physical boundaries to mental ones, from tactics or procedures to thought.

Awareness. Consideration. Engagement.

He drew three concentric circles—the structure of Leadspace Leadership.

Awareness – seeing what others miss.

Consideration – orienting yourself to Leadspace Leadership components.

Engagement – your energy in motion to transform awareness into action.

"Awareness is your radar, your outer ring," he said. "It's PICTURE—the habit of asking the right questions before reacting.

Purpose. Issue. Concepts. Time. Use of assumptions. References. Evaluation."

He smiled. "Top Gun fans might remember the call over the radio when Maverick calls 'Picture'—that same idea applies here. It's the disciplined communication that turns chaos into clarity."

He tapped the middle ring.

"Consideration is orientation. It's how you align yourself with others—connecting human capital and social capital. You saw it in CONNECT, BUILD, and DRIVE: relationships, responsibility, and roles."

He marked the center ring.

"Engagement is where it all moves. It's ACT, FACT, IMPACT—the rhythm of doing, grounding, and learning.

That's your leadership in motion."

Scholar-Practitioner Leadership

He stepped back from the board. "Leadspace Leadership didn't come from just any research," he said. "It emerged from my qualitative research and conversations with executive leaders responding to natural disasters."

He gestured to a slide showing his dissertation:

'Leadership in Defense Support of Civil Authorities – A Qualitative Exploratory Study.'

"The study drew on nearly a century of executive-level leadership during disaster response. From that work came the *Interdisciplinary Theory of DSCA Leadership*—empowering leaders, both military and civilian, to act with dynamic capability under pressure. Leadspace Leadership awareness grew from those findings—the art of sensemaking in motion."

He smiled at the group. "In plain terms—it's how leaders focus their time and energy into complimentary components to listen, learn, and lead when it matters most."

Articles of Engagement

He advanced the next slide:

ACT – FACT – IMPACT

"These are your *Articles of Engagement*," he said.

"It's the way I learned to write evaluation performance statements in the service, yet its application towards interactive adult learning is a true example of scholar-practitionership of leadership development.

What was the act?

What were the facts?

What was the impact?"

He wrote the words across the board.

"**ACT**—your topic of discussion.

FACT—your grounding knowledge.

IMPACT—your application of 'How'."

He paused.

"This isn't an academic exercise. It's accountability with purpose—your feedback loop for listening, learning, and leading."

The Kinetic Leadership Model

He turned to the final diagram—two interlocking pie wheels.

"The left wheel represents the *supporting discipline*—developing human capital: critical thinking, decision making, and problem solving.

The right wheel is the *supported discipline*—developing social capital: relationships, responsibilities, and roles."

He traced the connection between them.

"Together, they let you discover and explore your Leadspace Leadership.

It gives you a compass, not just a map—guiding you through the fog of leadership when the path isn't drawn but must be created."

He looked around the room.

"You'll learn to navigate both: the human and the social, the internal and the external, the self and the system."

Leadership as Energy in Motion

He erased the board and wrote one word: Energy.

"Think of your leadership as an energy discipline. Where do you spend your time, your energy?," he said quietly.

"Every conversation either generates it, redirects it, or drains it.

People don't follow titles—they follow your energy: your clarity, your confidence, your credibility."

He smiled at the commander.

"You set the tempo for courage."

To the administrator: "You manage the rhythm of care."

To the attorney: "You sustain the energy of trust under the law."

To the student: "You choose where your learning flows and goes."

"That's leadership," he said. "Energy—in motion—toward purpose."

Exploring Your Leadspace Leadership

He placed the marker down.

"Leadspace Leadership isn't something you memorize," he said. "It's something you discover and explore."

He let the room settle—that calm, electric stillness before a mission launches. Then he smiled.

"When you truly explore your Leadspace Leadership," he said, "you'll find that leadership isn't about rank, role, or recognition.

It's about awareness, consideration, and engagement—your ability to sense, orient, and move energy in ways that make a difference."

He paused, then leaned forward slightly.

"So ask yourself the real question—not the easy one, but the one only *you* can answer:

How do you know?

Not your spouse.

Not your boss.

Not your friend.

You.

How do you know that you're being the most effective leader you could possibly be—that you've done everything within your knowledge, skills, and abilities to be the best leader you can be?"

He let the words hang there weightless but undeniable.

The room grew still, not with hesitation, but with paused excitement.

A shared understanding filled the space, the awareness that leadership isn't measured by titles or tasks, but by transformation—within yourself and those you lead.

He smiled, quietly satisfied.

"Leadspace Leadership Certification," he said, "isn't just about proving knowledge, skills, or abilities. It's a declaration—that you've learned to thrive in complexity, to think critically, decide clearly, and move intentionally."

He looked around the room one final time.

"And that's what Leadspace Leadership is all about—being able to make sense of it all by communicating, connecting, and discovering the '*HOW*' to put your energy in motion to lead that creates clarity."

The room stayed silent—not empty, but full. Full of clarity. Full of energy. And as that energy rose quietly between them, Leadspace Leadership had finally done what it was always meant to do—allow everyone to realize their full potential as leaders.

CONCLUSION

LEADSPACE LEADERSHIP IN YOUR HANDS

Your Energy in Motion to Lead with Clarity

Leadership is not a title, position, or event.

It is an evolution—the movement from awareness through consideration to engagement.

Every framework, every lesson, and every reflection in this book leads to one unshakable truth:

You already possess everything you need to lead effectively and be the best you can possibly be, you just need to discover it.

The challenge is not in acquiring leadership—it is in *activating* it to navigate our world.

Leadspace Leadership is your compass.

It orients your thinking, centers your presence, and puts your energy in motion to lead with clarity, confidence, and credibility.

Awareness—Seeing What Others Miss

Awareness is where every great leader begins.

It is the discipline of perception—the courage to pause, to sense, and to see beyond the obvious.

Awareness helps you interpret the environment, understand complexity, and recognize patterns others overlook.

It transforms observation into insight and prepares you to lead with empathy and precision.

Awareness reminds you that clarity doesn't appear in silence—it's created by leaders willing to *listen longer* than others are willing to talk.

Consideration—Orienting Yourself to Leadspace Leadership Components

Consideration is the bridge between seeing and doing.

It's the inner orientation of a leader - the moment you align your values, intent, and awareness with the frameworks that shape Leadspace Leadership.

Through the frameworks you've explored—PICTURE, FIRESIDE, DEBRIEF, CONNECT, BUILD, DRIVE, ACT, FACT, and IMPACT - consideration becomes your method of sensemaking.

It helps you organize thought, manage pressure, and connect ideas into action. It's not about control, it's about connection.

Connection is how you translate awareness into understanding—the architecture of disciplined thought that allows you to act with confidence and credibility.

Engagement—Your Energy in Motion to Transform Awareness into Critical Action

Engagement is where leadership becomes kinetic energy - where thought becomes motion, and motion becomes impact.

It is the practice of putting awareness and consideration into movement.

Engagement is not about commanding others—it's about connecting them, aligning energy toward shared purpose.

When you engage with clarity and consistency, your leadership becomes contagious.

People feel it, not just hear it.

They move, not because they're told to, but because they're inspired to.

That is your energy in motion to lead with clarity.

The Call Forward

Now the question is when will you decide to discover your Leadspace Leadership?

Leadership doesn't wait for the perfect moment—it begins the instant you choose awareness over assumption, consideration over reaction, and engagement over hesitation.

Leadership does not belong to the chosen few.

Leadership belongs to the courageous many who are willing to stand in the fog and say,

"I can make sense of this."

This is your moment.

Because leadership isn't just what you do—it's how your energy changes the world.

Discover your Leadspace Leadership and put your energy in motion to lead with clarity, today!

Become Leadspace Leadership® Certified.

Visit www.leadspaceleadership.com to begin your journey.

PART IV

RESEARCH FOUNDATIONS OF LEADSPACE LEADERSHIP - A QUALITATIVE EXPLORATORY STUDY

The Scholar–Practitioner Origins of Leadspace Leadership

Leadspace Leadership is informed by qualitative research examining leadership performance in complex, high-stakes environments. The section that follows summarizes the scholarly foundations that shaped the framework and illustrates how lived experience, qualitative inquiry, and leadership science converged to inform its development.

While not required to apply the framework effectively, the research context presented here demonstrates why clarity through sensemaking—not experience alone—emerged as the defining capability of effective leadership in complexity.

Origins in Scholarship and Practice

My journey into this research did not begin in a classroom or in the quiet comfort of academic reflection. It began in hurricanes, wildfires, tornadoes, and oil spills—during the moments before, during, and after crises that tested leaders responsible for disaster response and recovery.

Supporting Defense Support of Civil Authorities (DSCA) missions for more than a decade revealed a consistent truth: even highly capable leaders—experienced, committed, and well-intentioned—were often overwhelmed by the environments they were tasked to lead. As complexity surged, data multiplied, and time compressed, clarity became increasingly difficult to sustain.

Across missions and agencies, one question repeatedly surfaced:

How do leaders make sense of overwhelming environments, and why do some leaders thrive while others barely survive?

This question became the catalyst for formal inquiry. I entered the study as a practitioner seeking to understand the cognitive, relational, and structural forces shaping leadership performance under extreme conditions—particularly in environments where decisions carried immediate and consequential outcomes.

Research Approach

To understand how leaders made sense of complexity—not simply what decisions they made—exploratory qualitative research provided the most appropriate methodology. Leadership in high-risk, time-compressed environments cannot be meaningfully reduced to metrics alone; it must be explored through lived experience, reflection, and meaning-making.

The study employed semi-structured, in-depth interviews with senior DSCA leaders representing emergency management, homeland security, defense operations, and multi-agency coordination. Participants possessed decades of experience and were responsible for decisions affecting entire regions, organizations, and populations.

Analysis was conducted using an inductive, scholar–practitioner lens informed by:

- Sensemaking theory
- Cognitive load and complexity research
- Functional role theory
- Critical thinking and decision-science literature

This approach allowed patterns to emerge directly from participant narratives rather than being imposed by pre-existing leadership models.

Emergent Leadership Themes

The analysis revealed **six interconnected themes** that consistently shaped leadership effectiveness in complex environments. These themes reflect the lived leadership experience within DSCA operations and align directly with the capabilities required to lead through uncertainty.

Critical Thinking

Effective leaders demonstrated the ability to slow down – take time cognitively, segment complexity, and identify what was possible rather than becoming consumed by what was happening. One senior leader described this capability as:

"We should do a better job of senior leaders, of all leaders, but especially at the operational, strategic level, to stop and think."

Critical thinking emerged as the cognitive anchor for all other leadership functions.

Decision Making

Participants described decision making as an ongoing sensemaking process rather than a single event. Leaders continuously integrated new information, consulted trusted colleagues, and adjusted decisions as environments evolved. As one leader noted:

"You may not have thought of it before, you've got to be open to learning from others."

Decision effectiveness was less about speed alone and more about clarity under pressure.

Problem Solving

Leaders emphasized adaptability over rigid adherence to doctrine. Effective problem solving required meeting challenges as they existed—not as plans anticipated they would. One participant summarized this tension succinctly:

"It's true sausage making. We identify the problem, look at the alternatives, and help them make a decision."

Relationships

No leader operated independently. Trust-based relationships enabled coordination across agencies and allowed decisions to move at the speed of need. As one executive leader stated:

"There's no complex problem you solve today where co-production of outcomes isn't required."

Relationships functioned as the operational lubricant that enabled clarity to translate into action.

Responsibilities

Clarity of responsibility—both one's own and others'—proved essential. Leaders who understood ownership boundaries reduced friction, duplication, and delay. A participant emphasized:

"I think if you have people working together who respect the roles and responsibilities that each agency has, it can be an amazing thing, but when they don't, it's really troublesome."

Roles

Leadership was experienced as a functional role requiring deliberate development and continual adjustment. Leaders described the need to shift between directive and collaborative roles as conditions demanded. As one leader reflected:

"At some point, complexity becomes circular, where it defeats existing legal frameworks, doctrine, standard operating procedures, and concept of operations - that requires a different set of skills."

Key Findings

Across all six themes, one insight emerged with unmistakable clarity:

Leadership effectiveness in complexity is determined by clarity—not experience alone.

The research revealed that:

- Cognitive overload suppressed critical thinking
- Overreliance on doctrine limited adaptability
- Fragmented communication hindered decision effectiveness

- Weak relational structures slowed coordination
- Role confusion created operational delays

Leaders needed a conceptual space to process complexity before they could create clarity for others.

Bridge to Leadspace Leadership

Leadspace Leadership emerged directly from these findings. Each research theme informed a corresponding word that represents a mental-model exercise to communicate through the noise.

- **Critical Thinking → PICTURE**
- **Decision Making → FIRESIDE**
- **Problem Solving → DEBRIEF**
- **Relationships → CONNECT**
- **Responsibilities → BUILD**
- **Roles → DRIVE**

Participants were not describing abstract leadership attributes. They were articulating the capabilities, the answer they wished they had when complexity surged.

Leadspace Leadership became the answer.

Summary

The "Leadership in Defense Support of Civil Authorities Operations: A Qualitative Exploratory Study" establishes the scholarly foundation that shaped Leadspace Leadership.

Leadspace leadership is backed by extensive research drawing from ~100 years of executive leadership experience responding to natural disasters. The result is a groundbreaking "Interdisciplinary

Theory of Leadership", empowering leaders from both military and civilian backgrounds to employ dynamic capabilities to thrive, not just survive.

The disasters and emergency operations set the stage, but it was the voices of experienced executive leaders, responding to natural disasters, that revealed what clarity truly requires.

The six themes—Critical Thinking, Decision Making, Problem Solving, Relationships, Responsibilities, and Roles—form the empirical backbone of the Leadspace Leadership framework.

The research confirms one essential truth:

Leadership is not the absence of complexity—it is the disciplined ability to create clarity within it.

Leadspace Leadership is built on that truth.

ACKNOWLEDGEMENTS

Throughout life, we encounter two kinds of people. The first are those who look into your cup to see if you have enough, because they genuinely care. The second are those who look into your cup to see if you have more than they do. This work exists because of the first kind.

It is with sincere gratitude, respect, and appreciation that I acknowledge the many individuals who have contributed to my growth as a leader, scholar, practitioner, and person. We've all heard the phrase, "standing on the shoulders of giants." Our learning and growth happen because others came before us, invested in us, and helped us see further than we could on our own.

In my experience, the mentors who shaped me never let me stand still. Instead, they extended a humble hand—guiding, encouraging, and sometimes pushing—because they saw possibility in me long before I could see it myself.

To my family and friends, whose love, patience, and belief have been constant sources of happiness and strength, thank you for supporting this leadership journey and the man behind it. Your encouragement and love make this work possible.

To my military teammates, students, colleagues, and leaders across every chapter of my career, you helped shape the ideas in these pages through shared experiences, honest conversations, and the responsibility of leadership in real moments that mattered.

To my mentors and teachers, you modeled what it means to lift others up. Your example continues to guide how I approach leadership development and service to others.

I cannot name every person who influenced this journey, but I hope to honor you by continuing the cycle you started. Be that person for someone else. Lift others up. Inspire people to pursue their passions and discover what is possible.

Every moment gives us a chance to choose: to lead, to grow, and to help others do the same. Take those chances. Make them your own.

Comments about Leadspace Leadership Certification:

"Leadspace leadership really made a difference for me. I've learned how important it is to keep the big picture in mind, especially when problem-solving and setting realistic timelines for getting things done. When people feel heard and supported, they're more likely to do their best work, which leads to better results for everyone."

"I have thoroughly enjoyed Leadspace Leadership. As someone who uses critical thinking a lot in their career, I loved being able to break it down into different parts. I could easily identify what I do well as a leader currently, and what tools I can use to better my leadership skills."

"Hearing the perspectives of so many different people from so many different backgrounds. It challenged me to think outside of the box and outside of what I'm used to doing. It also taught me to slow down when making decisions, take time, assess the situation, and work through it."

"Getting a different perspective on multiple aspects of leadership. New tools to use back with unit and personal life."

"I've learned several things that I have applied to not only leadership but my daily life with family."

"The dialogue - extremely valuable, insightful, and straight forward."

"Great at presenting concepts to navigate complexity and build relationships in a way that was accessible and applicable."

ABOUT THE AUTHOR

Dr. Caesar Kellum, USAF Weapons Officer (Retired)

Dr. Caesar Kellum is a retired United States Air Force Intelligence Weapons Officer with 27 years of service, where he learned firsthand about leadership clarity determining mission success. As both a Senior Noncommissioned Officer Enlisted Weapons Controller and an Intelligence Weapons Officer, he employed critical thinking, decision-making, and problem-solving tactics to lead effectively under pressure. His distinguished career includes earning recognition as one of the Twelve Outstanding Airman of the Year for the U.S. Air Force and serving the mission of the 601st Air Operations Center and First Air Force.

A scholar-practitioner of executive leadership and a Walker Fellow graduate from the University of Charleston's Doctorate of Executive Leadership, Dr. Kellum integrates decades of operational experience and academic insight into one powerful truth: leadership is energy—and when put in motion with awareness and purpose, it transforms everything it touches.

Through Kinetic Leadership Consulting, Dr. Kellum helps organizations and individuals across industries develop leaders who can think critically, decide with clarity, solve complex problems, and build trust in uncertain environments. He is the architect of the Leadspace Leadership Certification, a scholar-practitioner framework recognized by multiple professional boards and institutions, including Florida, West Virginia, and Louisiana Bar Associations for Continuing Legal Education (CLE) credits.

Alongside establishing Kinetic Leadership Consulting, Dr. Kellum has served as an Adjunct Professor at the University of Charleston's School of Business and Leadership and Gulf Coast State College Corporate College, where he designed and delivered courses on critical thinking, decision-making, communication, and team building. His civilian and academic leadership roles continue to reflect his lifelong commitment to developing leaders through discovery of how they can be the most effective leaders in our world today.

Dr. Kellum's professional and academic contributions include authoring the registered copyright work of Leadspace Leadership and publishing in The Journal of Total Rewards, Third Quarter 2022, pages 61–71 "Developing Critical Thinking in Leaders". His doctoral dissertation, Leadership in Defense Support of Civil Authorities Operations: A Qualitative Exploratory Study, explores leadership in high-stakes, dynamic environments.

When not teaching or speaking, Dr. Kellum mentors veterans, partners with universities, and collaborates with business leaders to expand the movement of Leadspace Leadership—helping people discover "How" to put their energy in motion to lead with clarity.

www.ingramcontent.com/pod-product-compliance
Lightning Source LLC
LaVergne TN
LVHW090529110826
845146LV00003B/1031